REAL WORLD SELLING STRATEGIES
THE ART OF THE SELLING CONVERSATION

BY HAL THORSVIG & JAMES HAYDEN

PREFACE

Why would anyone want to read another book touting successful selling techniques? Hasn't just about everything that could be written about selling success been written? Or so it would seem from the volume of available material on bookshelves that suggest how to sell yourself to others, or how to understand a prospect's reason for buying, or determining the decision makers. And it hardly ends here. Every imaginable sales situation has been diagnosed and dissected countless times and numerous approaches to solutions applied. Yet are you any further ahead in your career as a salesperson? How is your close ratio? Are you earning more business or losing more business? Are you and your sales team wasting time trying to follow up on sales that just don't close? How accurate is your sales pipeline?

So what IS new here? And what would entice someone… you… to purchase another "business success" book?

Our goal is to dispel past selling myths and ineffective sales techniques that are rampant in the business world and which cost companies millions of dollars of revenue in lost sales and under-performing customers.

Our book is based on the concept that PEOPLE buy. We will give you and your organization a common selling language and communication approach that will support you in developing and implementing strategies to close prospects, revitalize non-performing customers, and close business that has stalled. And though it is possible that you may stumble upon this approach after years of trial and error, you may take the fast track and read this book. You'll discover that our techniques have a broad base of applicability that enable you to become highly effective in the full scope of your business and personal life. Let this book take you to the top of your game.

Special thanks to our wives Kathy Thorsvig and Signy Hayden for massive support and encouragement during four years of writing this book. To Brad Mathews, who introduced us, for his valuable input and story in the ERB chapter.

Contact: james.hayden@comcast.net

Table of Contents

Preface

Chapter 1

Introduction

How often have you ended a sales phone call or left a sales call completely satisfied that you have engaged a viable prospect? Or is a more likely scenario one where you question what you could have said or done differently? Do you wonder if you should get back to the prospect or wait for the prospect to get back to you? Did you feel as though you left a good impression? Did you handle the prospect's questions appropriately? When I pose these questions to salespeople, the expressions on their faces indicate that, "yes, this happens to me." And as they look around, they see from the expressions on the faces of their colleagues that they are not alone.

We don't want salespeople to be left questioning the impact of their initial sales contacts. We certainly don't want a sense of confusion to linger in the mind of the salesperson. The bigger question that needs answering is, "How can I, as a salesperson, conduct an initial sales call feeling totally satisfied that this contact will most likely produce the business I'm hoping to obtain?"

The simple answer is control. Simple… yes: however, who is or who should be in control? The prospects? The salesperson? No question, the salesperson manages control of the selling process, and my objective is to teach you, the salesperson, to control the selling process to become the stellar salesperson you know you can be.

Managing control of the process and managing to stay in front of the prospects requires an understanding of the communication that occurs during the sales call.

What does controlling the selling process have to do with communication? Do we try to out talk the prospects? Do we wait for a pause in the conversation so that we can quickly jump in with our presentation? Do we merely defer to the prospects and allow them to direct the conversation?

Therapists have long suggested that every form of human communication involves a search for control by both or all parties. And this desire for control begins early in life. It can be subtle or not so subtle. Picture, for example, a mother trying to talk a two-year-old into eating a meal instead of playing. The adult decides it is lunchtime. The child continues to play. Food enticements are introduced. The child shows no interest. More play time after lunch is dangled as a reward. Still, no response from the toddler. So with a swift motion, the mother scoops up the child and plops him at the lunch spot. It took some patience and subtlety but the objective is met and the parent maintains control. An experienced parent understands the toddler's need for control and also understands the responsibilities of the parent. A less-experienced parent may end up exasperated and with an unhappy toddler if, during the exchange, the child is allowed to control the situation.

Though we are not comparing a toddler to a prospect or a salesperson to an exasperated parent, this example illustrates how early in life our search for control is introduced.

Like the experienced parent, the stellar salesperson knows how to manage or control the specific selling situation. A less-experienced salesperson is more likely to let control go to the prospect. How does this happen? I developed a diagram to help you understand exactly what occurs when a prospect controls the selling situation. I label this diagram the Universal Buying Process because it describes what will ALWAYS occur when a prospect controls the selling situation.

The diagram below illustrates the starting point for the 1st step in the process, the greeting or rapport step where both parties are on the same track.

THE PROSPECTS

RAPPORT

The prospect and salesperson both use the greeting as a rapport-building stage. Each works to make a connection. Conversational chitchat develops a common ground for questions and answers. But when the salesperson asks about problems, the prospect denies any.

What has happened? Didn't the salesperson establish

rapport? Doesn't the prospect want to solve a problem?

Check the diagram and you see that the prospect

advances to the 1st step of the Universal Buying Process,

denial.

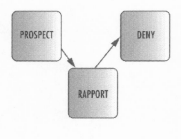

PROSPECT DENIAL

Let's take a step back. The prospect has just denied any problems within the company, and the salesperson is stuck wondering what it is he's doing here again. There are a number of reasons for prospect's denial. A prospect risks exposing a vulnerable area within the company if an issue is revealed. Perhaps he, himself, feels vulnerable. Prospects may also see salespeople as slick, dishonest, and perhaps liars. Not a positive image for the salesperson. But it is likely a salesperson who fits one of these descriptors has done business with the prospects, making the prospects now wary of all salespeople.

There are many examples of prospect's denial of a problem. The following narrative illustrates one.

A well-known Japanese company had rolled out a new product in Japan and had announced a rollout of the same product in the U.S. within the next six months. It was just at this time that our technology consulting company had an initial meeting scheduled with them. We had information that calls and emails to customer service in Japan had brought down the customer service system or CRM system in Japan, creating widespread customer dissatisfaction. If we could sell them our CRM solution for the U.S. market, they would have satisfied customers and be able to support a large sales volume. This was a great opportunity for our company. I contacted the prospects to discuss our CRM solution for U.S. customer support. The prospects immediately denied there was a problem, claiming there was no support issue and that their company was more than ready to roll out the new product in the U.S. conversation over!

Why did the prospects deny the existence of the customer support problem? What motivates prospects to deny obvious or exposed problems? It is a deeper desire to conceal or shield the company's or the prospect's true circumstances. Why does this happen? We as individuals tend to make decisions according to our own best interests. The prospects intend to control what is best for them and/or their company. From the prospect's perspective it is not in their best interest to reveal a problem that exposes an area of vulnerability within the business. Vulnerability implies weakness and the opportunity to be taken advantage of by a salesperson. A person in control cannot be weak.

Did the Japanese prospects make a decision according to their or the company's best interests? Yes, if you understand the company's wish to not appear lacking, regarding control of the customer support system. They chose to deny a problem existed even when evidence pointed to the contrary. Prospect denial gives control to the prospect, allowing the prospect to feel less vulnerable.

Now what? Does the sales call end here? Possibly, but you may find the prospect continues to express interest in the salesperson's product or service as part of the attempt to maintain control in the sales call.

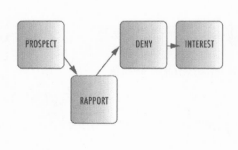

PRODUCT INTEREST

Questions from the prospects are a good sign to the salesperson.

The prospects may be truly INTERESTED and truly in need of your solution. Your solutions are a fit for their company. So, in an attempt to satisfy the prospect's interest in your product, you provide them with your features and benefits presentation. You even offer up a price quote and, the prospects, armed with enough information about your solution, are now able to compare you with your competitors and perhaps strike a deal with them. And, after all of this, the prospect was able to do this for free because you offered up a solution. Product information comes with a price for both you and the prospect. The cost to you…steep; the cost to him…free.

Here is a lesson in unqualified product presentation. It is a reminder of the cost to the salesperson of an unqualified presentation.

I sold incentive programs early in my career to technology companies. The programs were developed to entice the computer resellers to buy one company's product over another company's. I was working with a major player in the industry at the time and calling on them several times a week to set up an initial meeting. I received a call from the company telling me they were ready for an incentive program and I should come in to make a presentation.

I met with the Chief Marketing Officer and other executives. I ran through our capabilities, took their questions, and heard their compliments on our company's experience and my presentation. One of the executives asked, "What differentiates your company from the competition? What's your secret sauce? How do you do it? What would you design for us, tell us, and that will help us to make a favorable decision?"

Excited for the opportunity to close as my first sale such an important one, I proceeded to the whiteboard and presented our solution. We agreed to touch base the following week, but two weeks passed before I was able to reach someone at the company, and this is what I heard.

"Oh, yeah. I've been meaning to call you. We like you and your company. But we are some of the smartest people here in the world. Your programs are not rocket science, and now we can do this on our own, so we are moving forward with our own incentive program. Thanks for everything. Have a nice day."

Not the conversation I expected to have, but it was a lesson well learned. Do not ever present product information to an unqualified prospect!

ENTHUSIASM

Why do salespeople continue tossing their pitches to the prospects? The prospects throw out compliments to them on their superior product and product knowledge. The price quote is fabulous. The prospects imply future business is in the works. What a great salesperson you are. And who doesn't enjoy a compliment! It is easy to become caught up in this moment of mutual enthusiasm. It seems like the perfect sale, yet do you actually have the sale? Think of the number of times you have bought dinner for a prospect, discussed company business, worked to develop a good business relationship, and still not seen business materialize. The following story illustrates an experience I had relying on my rapport-building skills to solidify a business deal.

Once again, early in my career, I met a young executive, around my age, working with a large forest products' company, who assured me my product was a perfect fit for his company and we should work well together. We went out for at least twenty meals and perhaps ten sporting events over a period of a couple of years. It seemed that we were always just on the cusp of business. But at the end of that time, still no business.

I was basing my business relationship with him on what I thought was his enthusiasm for my product and my ability to work with him and his company. Instead of being a true business relationship, the individual used me to acquire our product knowledge and enjoy the free meals and baseball tickets.

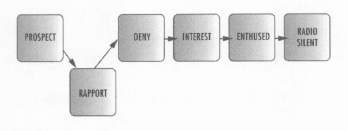

RADIO SILENT

For me as for most salespeople, it takes time to

process what happens next. It is usually an elated

salesperson who waits for the order to come in, still

thinking a sale is imminent. However, phone calls to the

prospects are not returned, and emails go unanswered.

What the salesperson sees as future business in the

pipeline is in fact inaccurate. When a prospect goes "radio

silent," the salesperson has less than a 10% chance of sales success. Most people don't like to say no. It is easier to ignore requests for a return email or phone call. It is the unqualified buyer's default to go Radio Silent.

We have all been here. In my 30 years of selling and working with sales people, I have determined there is not a salesperson working, including myself, who has not been caught up in the prospect's effort to control. Remember, in every communication process, each party searches for control. In a selling situation, it is the prospect's goal to control the sales process. If salespeople do not develop their own method to maintain control, they will always fall victim to the prospect's Universal Buying Process.

To combat this situation and give the salesperson a framework for staying on track, we define six factors that greatly influence the outcome of sales calls.

Understanding and successfully employing these factors will help to guarantee your success in maintaining control of the selling process. These six factors include:

1. Timing of the Greeting

2. Moment of Choice Question

3. Emotional Reasons for Buying

4. Buying Influences

5. Prospect's Financial Resources

6. Solutions

A successful salesperson controls the sales process…not the prospects.

THE SALESPERSON

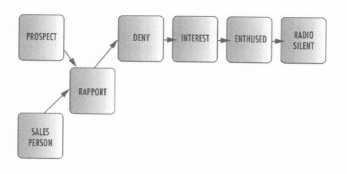

GREETING

Where does every sale begin? With the greeting and building a connection. An observant salesperson will connect with the prospect using simple clues gleaned from the office setting or the prospect's attire. Are there trophies on the wall, awards, family photos? Is the prospect dressed formally or casually? Small talk addressing any of these interests or life style clues is intended to develop mutual trust and interest in a very short time.

Salespeople today are selling in a global market or in a multitude of regional markets and all come with their own bonding rituals. While living and working in Texas, I could practically spend a day with discussions of bass fishing or hunting. In New York City and the major metropolitan East Coast areas, time spent on an introduction is more apt to be shortened to a nanosecond. Though obviously an exaggeration, my experience tells me that East Coast business people feel more rushed to get down to business. And while it is imperative that regional differences are noted, the salesperson must take the initiative in keeping the greeting period to no longer than 10 to 15 minutes.

If you find yourself spending more than 15 minutes, it is generally a sign of Call Reluctance, which means you would much rather stay for another cup of coffee and a donut and be in a feel-good moment, than take no for an answer. The fear of a "no" from a prospect translates into avoidance behavior, whereby the salesperson cannot or will not continue to call other prospects, and yet this is critical to the selling process. Allowing yourself to hear "no" from a prospect early in the game moves you more quickly to the next prospect. This way, time spent with the first prospect is not time wasted. The prospect has not succeeded in stealing time/money from the salesperson. The salesperson can move forward to the next call/prospect. Beat Call Reluctance by forming the habit of limiting the greeting period to 15 minutes.

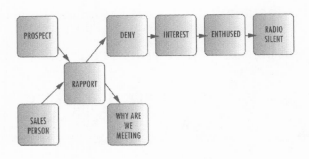

THE MOMENT OF CHOICE QUESTION

After taking a mental check on the time spent

building rapport, the salesperson poses the question;

"When you looked at your calendar and saw I was coming

in today, why did you choose to set our meeting?" This is

not usually what the prospect expects to hear, and now

instead of asking the salesperson "'What have you got?"' the prospect is given the opportunity to reflect on issues facing him or the company. It is safe to give specific information about the company's problems or needs instead of jumping behind a smoke screen of denial. Here, a salesperson is interested in fixing something specific as opposed to selling a one-size-fits-all program or product.

In traditional selling models, the salesperson is told to build rapport; offer up some features and benefits to create interest, and then close. By asking the prospects why they chose to meet, the salesperson will get an idea of the problems facing them. It is also an opportunity to move forward. But more importantly it is the Moment of Choice for the salesperson who intends to take control of the selling process.

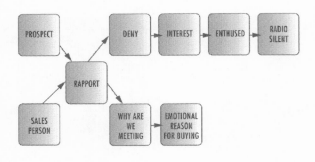

EMOTIONAL REASONS FOR BUYING (ERB)

The prospect's answer to the previous question may reveal one or more concerns. But the salesperson must dig deeper to determine the ERB or Emotional Reason for Buying. Why? Emotions tend to rule our buying behavior. Two emotions linked to buying behavior are pleasure and pain. It is easy to see this rule applied to the casual shopper who will often buy for pleasure, but in a business setting, ERB is the more intense emotion that drives prospects to buy. An awareness of this ERB forces them to take action now!

Those solutions/services the prospects' needs must be defined by the prospects' emotional attachment to those needs. In other words, the salesperson must help the prospects recognize that the ERB they are experiencing can be resolved by the salesperson's product/service. For now, understand that it is essential to identify. The "stellar" salesperson will gather enough information from the prospects to detect the real ERB and produce a product or solution for the ERB.

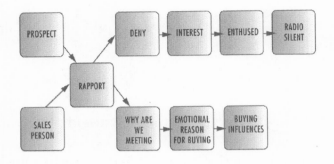

BUYING INFLUENCES

Reaching the person with the authority to actually approve the order can be a difficult process for many salespeople. Can the prospect say "yes"? Can he say "no" when everyone else has said "yes"? Does he have signing authority? For years I have worked with salespeople who spend considerable time presenting products or services that were well received only to discover that the prospects could not make the buying decision. I teach the salesperson to identify the various buying influences within the company. Understand them and you will reach the person with the signing authority!

I was selling incentives to boost market share and sales of semiconductors companies. The well-known company I approached saw its market share and sales chewed up by a competitor offering similar incentives to its distributors. My contact assured me that he was in charge of marketing and had responsibility and budget for my company's incentive program. It was as good as sold, according to the prospect. He was careful to control all contacts in the organization. I had not met with the executive team. And was assured that that wasn't needed. The contact merely needed a sign off from the executive team, who was in favor of our incentives, and it was a done deal. The business case yielded a 256 to 1 ROI, a no-brainer, and he said he had the executive team in his pocket on this one.

Several anxious days passed with no word from my passionate customer. Finally, a call. "Ahhh, some unanticipated news. Your program was killed by the CFO. Seems we need a new parking lot, and the fixed costs must go there. Sorry, we'll try again next year."

Clearly I did not research the Buying Influences.

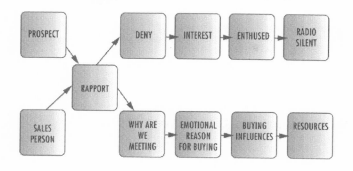

RESOURCES

Money issues in the selling process are reported by salespeople to be one of the most difficult areas to resolve. Why do we find ourselves backing away from talk about money? Could it be the social taboo that we just don't talk about money? Could it be the salespersons fear that if money comes up too early in the selling process, the prospects will back away? Actually, I think it is some of both. Our social mores restrict us from discussing personal money. Who asks their neighbors how much they make? We typically do not have conversations about our income or others' incomes.

In business dealings, it is the salesperson's job to confirm that resources are available, and only then are they able to move to the next step.

SOLUTION

When the prospect is qualified, the salesperson moves to the product or services that are available, or in other words, the Solution. At this point in the sales call, the salesperson has already confirmed the reason for being there, uncovered the pain, discovered the buying influences, and determined the resources. Now is the opportunity for the salesperson to produce the sales material and define the benefits of the products or services offered. How different is this sequence from the one in which the prospects controls the sale and acquires product knowledge in the initial stage of the selling process?

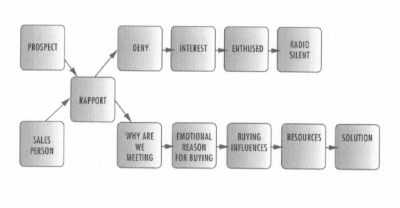

CONFIRMATION

The prospect wants the solution and agrees to purchase the product or service. The salesperson confirms the order and compliments the prospect's smart decision in making the purchase. Is the sale closed? NO! The salesperson can only consider the deal closed when the payment is received. We will learn in Chapter 9 a three-step prospect-confirmation process.

We have thus far outlined the various stages of successful selling, and in the following chapters we'll devote more time to each aspect of these stages of the selling process. The success or failure of a sale is often determined by the ability of the salesperson to control the sale. The choice is yours. Will you control the selling process or allow the prospects to control you?

Take a moment to review the diagram. Your "Moment of Choice" occurs in the initial stage of the selling process. You set the time limit for introductions and initiate the process with the first question. If you stay on track, you'll stay in control of the selling process.

You'll gain the respect of the prospects by empowering them to make the decision to solve their problems with your product or service.

Chapter Highlights

Chapter 1 Introduction

Need for control with the prospect and salesperson

Prospect

- Rapport
- Prospect denial: denying a problem exists
- Product Interest: presenting too early
- Enthusiasm: looks good

Salesperson

- Timing of greeting: limit time on rapport building.
- Moment of choice question: why did you choose to meet?
- Emotional reasons for buying: pleasure and pain. Both are the emotional reasons for buying
- Buying Influences: have you identified and met with all buying influences?
- Financial resources: have confirmation that resources are available.
- Solutions: discuss product or service/solution.
- Confirmation: reconfirm the order.

Chapter 2

Dynamic Positioning Statement

I was responsible for West Coast sales of loyalty programs directed to companies interested in frequent flier and frequent buyer campaigns. I had, finally, arranged a meeting with one of the big hotel companies wishing to put in place a frequent guest campaign. When the entire executive team including the chairman attended, I thought "WOW, all the decision makers are here; they must be very interested." Deciding they had done their investigative homework on our company, I was determined not to disappoint them. The inexperienced team I brought with me was eager to answer questions that arose. How do we track the company's performance? What do we name it? How do we communicate it? What is a ballpark of our fees? What are our formulas? Can you show us your samples? Excited at the prospect of a big sale, we eagerly proceeded to fill in all the blanks. We were going to sell our first major loyalty program.

The team and I left the meeting high fiving each other. Only after the excitement of the meeting had died down did I realize I didn't know their budget or if they were buying. I had neglected to ask about competitors. After weeks of trying to get in touch with the company, I made contact with the V.P. of Marketing who, after an awkward silence, told me that though our programs were great, they felt they could build the loyalty program themselves and save about $1.5 million. I lost control and spilled the GOLD again, and as a consequence lost an important and lucrative sale.

Haven't we all heard the old adage, "worth its weight in GOLD"?

From earliest times GOLD emerged as a commodity coveted and valued by individuals and nations. Its rarity and beauty created a desirability and fascination for all things GOLD, and so GOLD took on a power, giving it a place in history unlike any other commodity. Nations based economies on the GOLD standard. Ancient peoples identified GOLD with strength, power, and immortality. Consider the amount of GOLD found in tombs of the Egyptians. GOLD inspired legends and continues to be the medium used by jewelers to create our most precious and unique ornaments.

Though the GOLD standard is no longer the basis for our currency, it continues to function as the principal financial asset of many foreign currencies and governments and is held by central banks as a way of hedging against loans to their own governments as "internal reserve." GOLD coins and bars widely traded in today's market still serve as a private store of wealth for individuals. GOLD in our lives today continues to be a constant source of inspiration, valued and desired for its rarity.

You as a salesperson bring solutions to the marketplace as quantifiable as GOLD. Your solutions can impart power to businesses, allowing the business to increase sales, improve production, encourage creativity, and sustain market share. Businesses buying your solutions have the opportunity to stand above the rest and be envied for their successes in an ever-changing marketplace landscape. The salesperson becomes the player with the power when one considers the solution akin to GOLD, because your solution to marketplace issues can make or break many a business. Your GOLD is the desired commodity in a sales call. If the salesperson can see him/herself as the medium controlling the potential wealth of the prospect, then that person will control the sales call as well.

As the player with the power, consider how you would like to manage your GOLD. Does it make sense to offer it all up immediately? Do you think the prospect recognizes its value? Can the prospect offer you reasonable terms for your GOLD? Does the prospect even have a use for it?

Unfortunately, most salespeople fail to recognize the importance of the role they play in this scenario. When I ask salespeople, "Does your product or service bring considerable or even great value to the marketplace?" the response is invariably an emphatic, "Yes!" As a follow up, I ask, "Can your product or service solve the problems your prospects are experiencing?" Again they answer affirmatively. Finally, I ask, "Do you have any prospects who want your services/products without having to compensate you for it?" A predictably sheepish smile creeps over the faces of the salespeople. You can imagine their collective answers as they say, "Of course!"

What has happened here? The prospects have indicated a need for the marketplace solutions, acknowledged its value, and yet seem merely to be stringing you along. Is that their goal? Perhaps. Do they believe they can procure something for nothing? Possibly. Are you willing to unload all your GOLD early with a detailed explanation of your product/service, that is, offer them your solution to their problem for nothing in return? Most definitely not! How then, does the salesperson offer up a small nugget of GOLD to stay in the game without giving the game away?

Let's take a look at the Dynamic Positioning Statement or DPS.

Too often a salesperson will eagerly respond to the prospect's question, "What can you tell me about your product/service?" with a highly detailed explanation of the product/service offered. Isn't this just the opener the salesperson is waiting to hear? Now he can make his feature and benefit dump. After all, a competent salesperson will have a tremendous investment in product knowledge and benefits and will bring his enthusiasm for the product/service to the sales call and be all too happy to share this information with the prospect, imagining the perfect sale.

How can the salesperson prepare for this inevitable question? How much information should he/she provide? Is company history important? Are product information, sales testimonials, and name-dropping effective? Does the question need an answer?

Enter the Dynamic Positioning Statement or DPS. This is THE answer to the prospect's question for your company information. At the same time it opens the window of opportunity for a question-and-answer process with the prospect that leads to qualifying or perhaps disqualifying that prospect.

What is DPS? It is a statement that clearly defines the types of customers you work with, what solutions are available for your customers through your product or service, and a specific, third party report about the results your customers experience as a result of using your product/service. A DPS will tell the prospect WHO are your customers, WHAT you do for your customers, and WHAT are the RESULTS your customers report as a result of using your product or service.

A DPS example: "We work with business owners and executives, sales managers, and sales people to help them build their selling skills. Our clients report as a result of our program, sales increase up to 50%. Tell me about your company and what you do."

What is the REAL importance of the DPS? With a DPS in place, the salesperson avoids falling into the trap of an early, informal presentation of product/service benefits. With this statement, we have not told the prospect HOW we do something, simply what we do. Telling the HOW of the product/service is the beginning of giving away the GOLD.

With a DPS, the salesperson's company is differentiated from businesses using a formula statement to sell product/service benefits to the masses. How does the salesperson go about developing the DPS? Let's step back and take a look at the three basic elements of the statement:

WHO your customers are-

WHAT you do for your customers-

What RESULTS your customers experience when using your product/service-

Another benefit of a clearly rehearsed and succinct DPS is a link to the pulse of the marketplace. How does this fit with a DPS?

The marketplace is never static. Take for example a salesperson selling a product/service for more than ten years. Is that product/service the same today as it was ten years ago? Not likely. Is that person's DPS the same today as it was ten years ago? Again, not likely. When did the need to re-think their DPS get noticed? Probably when the information in the DPS no longer elicited interest from the prospect or worse, became inaccurate in the sales call.

The marketplace is dynamic and ever changing. Products and services become obsolete at the fastest pace in history, just as the horse and buggy went out of favor after the invention of the automobile. A cell phone today cannot compare to the cell phone of even a few years ago. Think of the DPS as an early warning system to alert us to subtle and sometimes not so subtle changes in the marketplace. Develop a Dynamic Positioning Statement, and continue to revise it dependent upon its relevance in your marketplace.

In the late 90's I was involved in working with business and technology executives with a solution that sorted out how to utilize their website to maximize their business and make more money. Over 90% of my clients asked us back for more work within a year.

Today there are tools that anyone can utilize to have a website presence, and websites can be built and operated in the hundreds of dollars per year rather than hundreds of thousands as it was eleven years ago.

What happened?

Social media was non-existent then, and now it is the fastest growing media available.

Blackberry's™ were new devices, yet most people now would not consider looking at video or an ad on a Blackberry™. The bandwidth of wireless connection speed was slow and the screens were poor.

Nineteen-year-olds are now able to develop websites, and there is a lot more to communicating on the Internet now with the proliferation of social media and mobile apps and websites.

Did you know in June 2011, it was reported that there is more communication through mobile apps than the Internet? Being an Internet expert these days isn't so valuable; being an expert about mobile phones is key.

My statement today:

I work with top brands and advertising executives to develop and implement mobile advertising. My clients report they make more money than they expected with the mobile applications because of our service.

A caveat: when selling highly complicated or technical products, eliminate buzzwords and technical jargon and terms that are typically understood by only a small segment of a company or industry. It is only confusing and possibly intimidating. A good adage when developing the DPS is to ask yourself how would I articulate my product/service to a seven-year-old child? It is surprising what clarity is brought to the picture when one is forced to tell a story in its simplest terms.

Chapter Highlights

Chapter 2 Dynamic Positioning Statement (DPS)

- Create a statement that defines:
    - Types of customers you work with.
    - Solutions available through your product/service.
    - Third-party experience/results with your product or service.

- Avoid telling how or a presentation. It spills the GOLD at this juncture.

- Update DPS at least every other year.

Chapter 3

MEETING AGENDA

In 1863, Henry Martyn Robert, a military engineer, was asked to chair a church meeting. Not pleased with his ability to lead the meeting, Robert decided to learn how to more effectively run a meeting and studied parliamentary procedures before developing a rulebook titled *Pocket Manual of Rules of Order for Deliberate Assemblies* that we know today as *Robert's Rules of Order*. How does this book connect with salespeople and selling? The author concluded that a successful business meeting should have an agenda that includes the order in which things occur, the subject matter, the time allotted for the meeting, and an initial agreement by the majority on changes that take place in the meeting. A sales call is a business meeting and therefore needs an agenda. This meeting agenda is an oral or written agreement between the prospect and the salesperson and will contain four parts.

1. Agreement on the desired outcome of the meeting for the prospect and review of the time allocated to accomplish the desired outcome.
2. Agreement for each party to share information relevant to the meeting.
3. Agreement with the prospect to decline your offer.
4. Agreement for ongoing communication between all pertinent Buying Influences and the salesperson.

We'll take a closer look at each of the four agenda parts of a sales call in the next few pages.

TIME and Outcome – STEP I

Rapport-building skills are a must for a salesperson, and even the most skilled can become caught up in the conversation while engaging a prospect. With good conversation, time flies, and when the prospect checks his watch to say time is up for him, the salesperson realizes, too late, that no business took place. The salesperson must establish before the meeting how much time the prospect will give to the business meeting. Giving the prospect the opportunity to set the meeting time allotment indicates a consideration for the time constraints we all face. The hours of the workday are equally distributed, and respecting the prospect's time is a valuable rapport-building component. In addition it gives the salesperson a clear understanding of the time he has to understand the prospect's problem. An effective "time" question is as simple as, "Thanks for agreeing to meet today. Do we have a hard stop or a set time to stop our meeting?"

With the time allotment agreed upon, next is an agreement on an outcome. In a stereotypical sales call, the features and benefits dump to create interest follows rapport building. This monologue by the salesperson is the hit or miss attempt to identify the prospect's true buying motives. Our method teaches the salesperson to focus on the prospect's needs with questions that will identify buying motives. And the first question deals with the outcome of the current meeting. "In our meeting today, if YOU had a perfect outcome, what would we have covered when it comes to my product or service?"

Where is the focus? On the prospects. At the outset, we focus on the prospects and what is important to them. Why do we do this? It allows you, the salesperson, to eliminate the guesswork by simply focusing on the prospects' needs, which is after all the reason you are here. The salesperson is here to get an understanding of the problem, because without knowledge of the problem the salesperson cannot be effective.

QUESTION – STEP II

The second step in the Meeting Agenda is to establish an agreement for each party to share information. The temptation is great for the typical salesperson to do a product demo or product pitch once the foot is in the door. However this style runs counter to our teachings. Skillful communication is still a valuable tool for the salesperson, but instead of taking the stage with product information, the salesperson communicates using a question-and-answer technique. The prospect typically waits for the product info, but we want to change this way of thinking. This may best be accomplished by getting an agreement that both parties share information. An agreement for both parties to share information provides the salesperson with valuable information about the company while at the same time allowing the prospects to identify the problem(s) for themselves.

REMOVE THE PRESSURE – STEP III

There is probably nothing worse than feeling as though you are being boxed into a corner, but that feeling is not uncommon among prospects, who agree to meet with a salesperson and then realize they don't want to be "sold." Perhaps the prospects have second thoughts about buying or simply want to hear what is new in the market and is now just trying to figure out how to say 'no thanks' to the salesperson. To avoid this situation, we introduce step three in the oral agenda: remove the pressure. We offer the prospects the opportunity to decline the offer. If they discover our offer is the solution, the salesperson must learn what kind of process the prospects will go through to buy the solution.

Why would a salesperson, at the beginning of the call, want to give the prospect an out? What is the advantage to the salesperson? Feeling boxed in puts the individual in a defensive position. Picture the prospect with hands up, warding off any further conversation. Is he in a comfortable spot? Probably not. Is there the likelihood the salesperson can have any meaningful communication that will advance the sale? Probably not.

But we can move him from defensive to comfortable by allowing him the opportunity to decline the offer. In doing this, the salesperson assures the prospect that he is not there to "take him to the mat."

ONGOING COMMUNICATION & BUYING INFLUENCES – STEP IV

Your prospects are moving closer to becoming clients, and Step IV in the meeting agenda will position them for becoming clients. At this point the salesperson and prospects agree to ongoing communication to follow this initial meeting. Without the agreement to follow up with email or voice mail, the prospects could easily fall into "radio silent mode." And no salesperson wants to find herself waiting by the phone or checking email to see if a deal is still alive. A clear statement dealing with open future communication between the salesperson and all buying influences is another essential ingredient to the four-step meeting agenda.

Early in my sales career, I sold enterprise-marketing solutions. A relatively new, rapidly growing company in the Seattle area had a reputation for hiring the "smartest people in the world." They were also known to have a load of cash. After six months of prospecting, I finally scored a meeting with the VP responsible for the marketing budgets. I didn't need to qualify her, as I heard from colleagues that she was the "one." I was sure she would see a need for the services I had to sell to her. Her only response was by email, which meant no phone contact with her prior to our meeting. And I was so delighted to have a meeting scheduled after months of asking for a meeting that I neglected to ask my typical questions of the Big Prospect.

- What marketing plans did she have for the next year?
- What are the big issues she was facing?
- Who else is involved in these types of initiatives and do they need to be included in the meeting?
- Why is she interested in meeting with me?
- What does success look like in a meeting?
- If it is a successful meeting, what will happen next?

I knew these questions were necessary for a successful first meeting, but for the Big Prospect I threw these questions out the window because our CEO was calling me every week about getting a meeting with this company. And hearing that I had the meeting, he let out 128 decibel Whoop!

Every ounce of my

being was crying out to be the star of the company; to be loved - to be the man. Every insecurity in my life came up. Why did my birthparents give me up? Why was I picked on in Junior High? Why didn't girls like me until I was well into high school? I was lucky as hell to be meeting with this woman; really, why should she meet with me anyway? Would she see me as the late-blooming, gawky nerd that was looking for love and validation through this meeting?

Wow! I felt I was lucky just to go to a meeting with her at this premier company. And I needed to add another big sale to the quarter to support my daughter's private school tuition and the new vacation home I acquired. This call will be fine; I am persuasive and I will wing it. She will buy.

The big day arrived, she confirmed a half- hour

meeting, and I was certain that she would be so enthralled by our product that she would meet with me for much longer. I was nervous on the drive to the company's suburban campus and was awed by the fact that she may be smarter than I am. When I checked in at the lobby and signed in on the computer, I was so shaky that I had a difficult time seeing the computer screen. Since I was early, I had time to run through the meeting in my head. After what seemed like quite a lengthy wait, the Big Prospect came through the door. I shook hands hoping she wouldn't notice how sweaty my palms were.

My nervousness showed through when I tried to win her over with my personal bonding questions. "Are you from Seattle? Cleveland, great – didn't a river catch fire there, or was that Detroit? So, how do you like the weather in Seattle? Yeah, that's why I have lived here most of my life." Thinking I was a dead man walking and hoping to turn this around, I noticed she had on a ring and asked, "Do you have children? Oh, you and your partner have decided not to have kids."

Now I felt as though I was walking to the execution chamber and wondered if I would have a last meal when she offered me a soda or coffee. I went for the water since my throat was so dry. Once in her office she reached behind the computer screen, grabbed a cooking timer, tick, tick, tick. She stated that I had 30 minutes and said she had a "hard stop." This was my first exposure to the term hard stop, and I thought, OK, I must tell her everything I know in 30 minutes. I proceeded to do just that. I could see how interested she was with the questions she asked, and I was sure if I told her everything, she would see how smart I was and then naturally buy from me.

The timer sounded, and she asked if I would send a soft copy of my presentation with our recommendations. When I returned to the office to call our CEO, doubt began to settle in. "Why would she buy? Does she have a budget? Is she in a position to buy? Why didn't I ask those questions?" But I promised to send out our recommendations so, pushing off a meeting with my biggest client; I followed up with the document. For the next two months, I attempted to contact the Big Prospect until one day I heard through the grapevine that the company was rolling out a campaign with a competitor just like the one we discussed in our meeting. My ideas, even the name of the campaign, were very close to my recommendations.

After several weeks, I received an email from the Big Prospect saying the company had decided to go with another company. This is outrageous, I thought. How can they execute their campaign with our company's ideas? Isn't that illegal? Or was I naive? How had I lost control of the sale? I realized I had not followed the sales process that we are advocating in this book. Like a losing sports team, I got away from my game plan, played by someone else's rules, and wasted a lot of time and money.

Here is the agenda from a pivotal sales meeting with the same company two years later that ultimately netted $2,000,000 in sales for our company.

Agenda:

- Allocate time for the meeting.

- Establish an ideal outcome.

The salesperson must establish before the meeting how much time the prospect will give to the business meeting. Giving the prospect the opportunity to set the meeting time allotment indicates a consideration for the time constraints we all face.

The next question deals with the outcome of the current meeting. "In our meeting today, if YOU had a perfect outcome, what would we have covered when it comes to my product or service?"

- Share information.

Establish an agreement for each party to share information. The temptation is great for the typical salesperson to do a product demo or product presentation once the foot is in the door. However this style runs counter to our teachings. Skillful communication is still a valuable tool for the salesperson, but instead of taking the stage with product information, the salesperson communicates using a question and answer technique.

- Say no or move forward.

Offer the prospects the opportunity to decline the offer. If they discover our offer is the solution, the salesperson must learn what kind of process the prospects will go through to buy the solution.

- If a good outcome:

a. Define and introduce to others involved.

b. Return e-mail and phone calls.

c. Say no at any time or discuss roadblocks.

At this point the salesperson and prospects agree to ongoing communication to follow this initial meeting. Without the agreement to follow up with email or voice mail, the prospects could easily fall into radio silent mode.

- Establish method for ongoing communications.

The party that controls the agenda will likely control the outcome of the meeting. I would encourage all salespeople to write their own meeting agenda in words that best fit their speech patterns and develop a standard format for a written meeting agenda. Put a copy next to the telephone. Carry it on a sales call and present it to your prospects. Use it! There is magic to producing a written document, and it places the salesperson in control. My clients tell me having a well-practiced oral or written Meeting Agenda is the single most distinguishing behavior to produce early improvement that forces results in their selling process.

Chapter Highlights

Chapter 3, Meeting Agenda

Agreement between prospects and salesperson and contains:

- Agreement on time allocated for the meeting and agreement on the outcome for the prospects.
- Agreement for each party to share information.
- Agreement for the prospects to say no or move forward.
- Agreement for ongoing communication between all pertinent buying influences and the salesperson.

Chapter 4

Emotional Reasons for Buying

It goes without saying that emotions play enormous roles in our lives, from our first great loves to our greatest fears. Emotions can be controlled or uncontrolled, strong or weak. Emotions motivate us for action or inaction. And in selling we look for those emotional motivators that cause the prospects to take action. Both pleasure and pain motivate an individual to action, but of the two, pain is by far the stronger motivator, and we'll examine this as a motivating factor for buying in a selling situation.

I need a new car. Or rather should I say I want a new car? I can picture myself driving to my next sales call in my new Black Luxury Sedan with all the bells and whistles. I don't really need a new car. The car I drive now is quite satisfactory, is mechanically sound, and gets me where I need to go. But I would feel so good driving this car, and wouldn't it make me look that much more successful? I begin to wonder if my old car makes a statement about my success or lack of it. Am I actually embarrassed being seen in my car?

With the vision of seeing myself driving down the street in my new car, I head to the dealership. I am greeted by a salesperson and tell him I'm thinking of getting a new car and would like to look around. But first, I start with questions about the various models. What type of engine does it have? How is the mileage? What comes with the warranty? Certainly these questions are relevant. But is this truly the reason I came to buy a car in the first place? No. My trip to the car dealer started with an emotional need to look more successful. I wanted to take away the *pain* of embarrassment. And now to qualify that need to erase the pain, I ask questions based on practical reasons to purchase. I would look rather silly asking the salesperson, how do I look in the car, but that question more accurately reflects the reason I am at the dealership in the first place.

The purpose of this story is to illustrate our reasons for buying, which are typically emotional reasons. It is embarrassing for me to appear less successful because of the older car I drive. I can relieve that embarrassment with the purchase of the car I really want to own. I can satisfy the intellectual need to purchase the new car with the questions I ask the salesperson. So on the strength of this ERB I buy a new car. In every sales situation, emotional reasons for buying significantly influence the sale.

Why is it that the pain of something motivates the buyer? We find that pleasurable experiences can often be delayed, but people will generally take action more immediately to avoid discomfort. How many of you have found a prospect spending money purely out of pleasure upon seeing a new product? Not likely.

If pain is the motivating factor for buying, how then, do we tap into this ERB?

To convey an understanding of the concept of emotional pain, I introduce the idea of fears and pose this question in my training session. "As humans, what do you suppose is our biggest fear?" Responses vary wildly, but they are always personal and emotional and often touch on the fear of death. Does this mean we greet our next prospect with, "I know you're worried about dying, so why don't you just go ahead and tell me what your problem is?" I don't think that will quite work, and it won't exactly build trust and rapport with the prospect! But the idea here is that fear creates emotional pain. So, in a sales call, how do we identify the specific fear or fears that create the prospect's ERB?

We have all had prospects question us on our products or services. And generally the questions are specific to their needs. These very specific questions represent an Early Warning Indicator or EWI and are used by the salesperson to determine just how emotionally engaged the prospects are with each of the underlying issues. Following is a series of questions recently asked by a prospect of a printing company.

- "What is the quality of your print service?"

- "What kind of technical support do you offer?"

- "Are your prices competitive?"

- "Is customer service readily available?"

- "Do you guarantee on-time delivery?

On the surface, these questions seem fairly straightforward. An inexperienced salesperson will answer them affirmatively and then proceed to a presentation of product information. A salesperson, using the EWI listens carefully, interpreting them quite differently. Though they all appear to be customer-related and surely can be satisfied with the salesperson's solution, the experienced salesperson sees the questions as an indication of an underlying problem (fear) facing the prospect. Many prospects have a fear of losing their jobs or a fear of not making enough money and all the possible repercussions that ensue. So we teach the salesperson to use an Early Warning Indicator or EWI.

These EWI questions present an opportunity for the salesperson to determine how emotionally engaged the prospect is with each of the underlying issues. That is, which item brought up by the prospect is causing the greatest discomfort? How do we tap into this discomfort to be able to offer a solution?

This diagram of an onion with its many layers helps to understand the process that occurs when a salesperson seeks to uncover the underlying problems causing the discomfort. As each layer of onion is peeled away, another layer of concern is revealed until the salesperson gets to the core of the problem. The five layers represent specific emotional levels that need to be reached before

the real ERB can be identified.

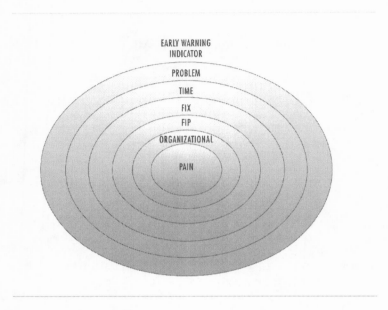

Each prospect's question about a salesperson's

product/service becomes an EWI trigger attached to the

outer layer of the onionskin. The questions indicate a

prospect's concern about a problem. It could be a

concern about service, product, tech support, or any

number of issues the prospects may have faced in the past or continues to face now.

We'll use our experience with the printing company prospect to support this idea as we peel away a layer at a time starting with the prospect's question, "Do you guarantee on-time delivery?"

P. "Do you guarantee on-time delivery?"

S. "And it's a problem?"

P. *Prospect has experienced a problem; 1st layer is peeled*

S. "And this has been an ongoing problem?"

P. *Prospect tells duration of a problem; 2nd layer is peeled.*

S. "What actions have been taken to solve the shipping problem?"

P. *Prospect discusses previous solutions for a problem; 3rd layer is peeled.*

S. "Are there any financial implications to this problem?"

P. Financial costs to prospect are listed;

4th layer is peeled.

S. "What might compel you to fix the problem?"

P. Prospect gives reasons to fix a problem; 5th layer is peeled.

S. If the problem is solved, how will that affect your organization?"

P. Effect of the problem on the organization and the prospect personally are discovered; 6th layer is peeled.-

When we view a cross section of the onion diagram, we can clearly see that it took us six questions to reach the prospect's pain. Let's analyze these six questions and note that the salesperson leads off with a comment intended to elicit more than simply a yes or no answer from the prospect. Why these questions? What sort of information do we hope to gain? How do we interpret and organize the information the answers reveal?

1st Question: Prospect experiences a Problem:

At the outer layer the salesperson picks an EWI trigger to confirm that a problem exists. Why? There is no reason to waste time continuing to discuss a non-existent problem, so the salesperson must choose another EWI question, if that is the case.

2nd Question: Duration of a Problem:

We want to know how long this problem has affected the prospect. Have delayed or late shipments been a problem for years? Months? If late shipments have persisted for years, there is a pretty good chance the prospect has learned to live with the problem. If it's a more recent issue, it's more likely that the prospect will take action to fix it. Understand the duration of the problem!

3rd Question: Solutions for the Problem:

If the salesperson can determine what fixes the prospect might have already tried that did not solve the problem, the salesperson will know what not to offer. As an added bonus, this question also reveals competitor information that is extremely useful.

4th Question: Financial Costs to the Prospect:

This is one of the key questions in peeling for pain. Does the prospect understand the cost of the problem? Can the prospect put into words, for example, the cost in lost sales from an under-performing salesperson?

5tth Question: Reasons to Fix a Problem:

Compelling reasons to fix the problem may be related to diminished brand value, lost market share, outselling by competitors, falling behind in technology, reduced margins, increased production costs.

6th Question: Effect of the problem on the Prospect:

The salesperson has reached the core of the onion. This is the true emotional reason for buying. The salesperson listens for emotional responses from the prospect that can include words of frustration, anger, worry, fear, loss, etc.

The following narratives illustrate an understanding of the ERB concept within the context of the sales call.

A Giftware Company

The first professional sales job I had was during the early economic downturn in the 80s. I was selling giftware to gift shops in Oregon and quickly realized that most of my buyers were hobbyists with slim budgets. One of the lines I represented was collectible clown statues, and the artist had come out with his biggest collectible piece to date; a carousel that was about eight feet in circumference. It was $5000 wholesale and $8000 retail. One of my customers, Dorothy, saw her shop as the premier place in the Northwest for clown collectors. This was her hot button. It was important for her to be seen as the Northwest leader in clown collectibles.

I had the photos of the carousel and made an appointment with Dorothy, who was operating on a small budget. I said, "Dorothy, I have a surprise for you, and before I leave today you must see something." First, I showed her some other giftware, and she bought a few things. I cautioned her to save her budget for the last item.

Her largest purchase from me in the past had yet to exceed $1000. I showed her the picture of the carousel and said, "Dorothy, can you imagine having a clown collectible that no one else in the Northwest will own?" She took a deep breath and asked, "How much is it?" "$5000," I said. She recoiled.

Oh, shoot, I thought, I'm losing her, and this is the only shot I have for this big sale, but I knew her hot button was being the premier source for clown collectors. So I suggested she come outside to the storefront and view the carousel picture in her front window. I said, "What will people say and think when they walk by your store and see the carousel in your front window? You will be seen as the Queen of Clown Collectors." Dorothy began to tear up and asked, "Where do I sign?"

Dorothy's emotional reason for buying was to be seen as having the best clown collection in the Northwest. For her, it was more important than price. So offering her a collectible that no one else had equaled success for Dorothy. Dorothy's self-image was tied to owning the most impressive collectible clown collection, and my realizing that led to the sale.

U.S. Truck Manufacturers

I was selling motivational programs in the mid-eighties with a national marketing group, and one of the biggest programs I had going was with a U.S. truck manufacturer. I had a great mentor and client there, and for several years we ran an incentive reward trip for truck dealers. After the first year, my client disclosed that he used the trips to maximize attainment of his yearly personal financial objectives; that is to receive a big bonus and take a vacation to a great location with his wife. After inviting my wife and me to join them on a Caribbean cruise and poring over other possible travel destinations, I understood his personal agendas and real reason for buying our solutions. I also discovered that my client had a big financial overhead with two sons in college and he needed our programs to make his bonus and ensure he was able to help pay for his sons' educations. I helped tailor our motivational programs for the client so that he was able to achieve his bonus compensation and in effect, provide for his sons' college educations and reward himself and his wife with incredible travel destinations. Based on his success, he was promoted to senior vice president, and a part of that success was continuing with our company's motivational programs.

U.S. Luxury Car Manufacturer

I am currently working with a company that sells advertising and sponsorships on mobile applications. We were producing a mobile application for a car magazine and had been presenting them to auto manufacturers. My client, one of the U.S. luxury car manufacturers told us their company wanted to be the launch or initial sponsor of one of the mobile applications. Several weeks had gone by, and no paperwork had arrived to firm up that sale. Then a European competitor began to show an interest. I warned the U.S. car company that this was going to sell with or without them and they needed to get the paperwork in if they wanted to be first to market. The U.S. team stated several times that they wanted to be first to market with this new technology to show market and technological leadership. The European team sent in the order and got the app launch and sponsorship. My U.S. client told us she would never let this happen again.

When it was decided to take a sister publication to market, we called the U.S. manufacturer first and told them this, too, would go fast. Two days later – sold!

The real reason the client bought wasn't money or budget. It was because of branding and perception. The U.S. manufacturer didn't want a competitor to be perceived as more innovative than their company, and they found budgets to prove that. Had they failed to take advantage of the opportunity to be perceived as an innovator, the marketing people at both the car company and the ad agency would have been fired. So in effect, they actually bought because of a fear of being fired.

Software Company

I was working a major trade show where heavy construction equipment and related products were shown. Many of the show attendees were from heavy construction companies. My company provides software that, among other things, helps construction companies manage their fleet of heavy equipment more effectively. A casually dressed man walked up to me in our booth and asked to see a demonstration of our software. I replied that I would be glad to show him our software. Then I said, " There isn't something causing problems in your business that you are looking to solve?"

He said that he was having problems with allocating equipment hours and costs of his equipment to jobs. I asked if he could be more specific, and he elaborated on some of the difficulties they have in charging equipment to jobs. He also mentioned that in some cases they might not be fully billing for some of the equipment expenses that they incur.

I responded with, "It sounds like these issues can be a nagging problem for you, but they aren't costing you any real money at this point. Just to pick a number this isn't costing your business, say, $10,000 a year?" He responded, "Yes, they do cost us money. In fact, the number is probably more like a half million dollars a year." Then he paused for a second and his eyes looked up and away as he redid the math in his head. "No wait, it's at least one million dollars a year."

He said this as if it were the first time he had really put the numbers together. He seemed rather analytical about it and the dollars didn't seem to matter all that much. So I asked him, "How do you feel about that number?" His expression changed to one of anger, he stepped forward a full step,

and got right in my face saying: "Pretty god damn bad,

I'm the owner of the company!" We spent the next twenty

minutes reviewing specific highlights in the software that

addressed these issues and agreed to schedule a full

software demo in the coming days. The software purchase

was concluded just a few weeks later for well over

$100,000.

Chapter Highlights

Chapter 4, Emotional Reasons for Buying (ERB)*

- Pain is the motivation.

- Ask questions to find pain

  - Is there a problem?
  - How long has it been a problem?
  - Have they considered these fixes?
  - What is the cost to the prospect?
  - What is the reason to fix the problem?
  - How is the prospect personally affected?
  - How is the organization affected?

Chapter 5

Buying Influences

Have you ever made what you felt was the world's best sales presentation only to learn the people you are presenting to could not make a buying decision? Did you find yourself stalled on a deal, not able to move forward because your prospect does not make purchasing decisions? And now you don't know where to go from here. Who controls the buying decision? How do you find that information? Quite simply, you ask for it. Just how you retrieve this information is the subject of this chapter.

Sales can be a frustrating profession, and nothing is more frustrating for salespeople than knowing they have a great product or service, are well-versed in product information, and find companies who can benefit from their product or service, but they cannot seem to reach the individual who really can say "yes, we want your product or service!" Understanding how to ask for the decision maker is a skill that continues to elude many competent salespeople. And if you don't learn this skill, you don't move forward.

This chapter is devoted to the Buying Influences. These are the decision makers, the players in the company who will make the decision to buy or not buy your product. It will be important to identify first the type of sale involved and then the types of individuals who have unique decision-making authority to confirm the purchase.

In my training, I describe two types of sales, the simple sale and the complex sale. The simple sale is defined by its lower dollar volume and typically faster sale. The product or service is lower cost and a mistake in buying the wrong service or product does not typically have far-reaching consequences. There are typically one to two decision makers. Purchasing toner cartridges is an example of a simple sale. The salesperson reaches one decision maker. If the product does not work out, the buyer returns it, or the salesperson substitutes another product or brand.

A complex sale involves a greater dollar investment and has typically more than two decision makers. Because the dollar volume is higher, more is at risk for the buyer. Layers of decision makers help create a cushion for the risk. Take for example an accounting software product that costs over $100,000. Money and time invested in conversion and training people makes it imperative that the decision to purchase is fully vetted. The selling cycle in a complex sale tends to be longer than that in a simple sale.

When working with complex sales involving several buying influences, you may find or already know an individual within the company or associated with the company that we call the Chauffeur. This individual becomes an all-important resource for you to gain the inside track to the buying influences. Imagine the familiar chauffeur of the movies, who is privy by default to the back seat deals of executives and is trusted for his discretion. Their job rests in finding the shortcuts or back roads to avoid congestion or sometimes more importantly to protect the interests of their employer/client. They learn the individual habits of their patrons and are able to foretell preferences and avoid conflict. As the name implies, your Chauffeur will have the inside track and information to help you navigate through unfamiliar territory. Your chauffeur will offer tips and information that will enable you to more easily identify the buying resources, pinpoint the specific objectives of each buying influence in the purchase and show you how to deliver a product/service that produces a mutual advantage for both parties. The Chauffeur has a vested interest in your and your company's earning the business. It is a mutually beneficial relationship.

For the sale in which there is no apparent Chauffeur to guide you, the salesperson must find the buying influences without this guide. To help with this process, I identify four Buying Influences. They called the Investigative Buyer, the Utilitarian Buyer, the Sensitive Buyer, and the Dominant Buyer.

The Investigative Buyer gathers products/services information. This person can be from positions as diverse as purchasing, IT, engineering, or operations personnel. This individual does not usually offer up company information but is interested in gathering new product/service information for the purpose of qualifying or disqualifying the product/service. Price plays a role in the decision to qualify or disqualify. The Investigative Buyer cannot, alone, say yes to a product/service, but this individual can help maneuver you through the buying process.

The Utilitarian Buyer is the actual user of the product/service. These individuals can be often overlooked as players in the selling process. Because they use the product, it is essential that they understand the benefit and how to use it. A company I worked for designed plastic collapsible bins for the automotive after-market. These bins were replacing metal bins, and the forklift drivers who handled the bins insisted that the plastic bins would simply not hold up in the loading process with the forklift. In order to sell the plastic bin, our company worked to retrain the forklift drivers in the loading process. Instead of the sale being sabotaged by the drivers who typically rammed steel bins onto a pallet, we trained them in a different loading method, which was far simpler and took less time.

The Sensitive Buyer is directly affected by the product or service. This individual or group in the organization measures the product or service by the consistency of productivity. For example, if a ball bearing on the line is replaced by a cheaper product, and that line breaks down when the bearing fails, the Sensitive Buyer suffers the consequences. If the product or service consistently produces good results, the Sensitive Buyer will move you more quickly through the buying process. Though the people in this position cannot say yes to you, they can overrule the Investigative Buyers, especially when productivity diminishes due to product/service quality.

In the case of selling plastic bins, the Utilitarian Buyer may be the head of shipping. In the case of a software customer service/ CRM solution, the Utilitarian Buyer may be VP of IT. The person you work with is dependent on the type of company and sale. If you need help sorting out just who the right buyer is for your project, contact us and we can help you.

Last is the Dominant Buyer. As is indicated by the title, this influence dominates every other buying influence involved in the buying process. This individual can be a manager, vice-president, president, COO, CEO, even a board member. This is the ultimate buying influence, and this individual can say yes or no to the purchase. Though these individuals may take into account the recommendations of the other Buying Influences, they ultimately hold the trump card. They can reject the product or service even when the others have said yes to you.

Now that we have their identities, how do we reach them without the aid of a Chauffeur? If your prospect alone is the only decision maker, you have no worries. You're in a simple sale. But even at that, what is the guarantee that you have reached the Dominant Buying

Influence? We teach salespeople to pose a direct question to the prospect, which will firm up the identity of the dominant Buying Influence and perhaps produce others.

If your prospect offers up no other Buying Influences and says he/she makes the decision, yet you are uncertain, a follow-up comment/question would be in order. These "soft" questions and comments to the prospect build on the trust and rapport already established, and it is much more likely that you will receive accurate information when using this technique. Many times I hear the prospects say they do run the decision by a boss, the president, board member, or committee.

How you reach these Buying Influences and just how many of these Buying Influences you communicate with personally will depend on the questions you ask of prospects and the information received from them. Even though a prospect may be a president, that individual may need or want to confer with others in the organization and perhaps may not wish to bring you into the mix. Committees can be especially threatening to upper management who don't wish to appear foolish or embarrassed if they cannot sufficiently answer their questions as to why your product/service is necessary to the company's operations. To avoid the problem of being kept out of the loop, I rehearse the prospect for the tough questions that may be asked regarding my products/services. By doing this, I gain a well-rehearsed prospect who will be an advocate for me if I'm not present. Or the prospect may simply invite me to meet with the other Buying Influences.

There will be times when you are working directly with a CEO or president and believe you have reached the Dominant Buyer. You may find that these individuals still take the purchasing process to another top management person. Titles don't always determine the Buying Influences. The buying process in a complex sale can have a number of twists and turns. To avoid pitfalls and the possibility of being misled by company titles, we developed questions for the prospects so that the salesperson can get a clear picture of the buying process within the organization.

- Do they have a specific buying process?
- Have they purchased a similar product/service before?
- If not, what would they have done had they been presented with a product/service such as this?

- What type of consensus is needed to make a decision to move the process forward?

- How long do they expect it to take?

- What is the latest date the project can be implemented?

- What might be an optimum date, considering the number of steps needed to go through the process?

- Which members of the buying influence groups can approve to move forward?

- Is there a committee? Members?

- Is one committee member more influential?

- Historically, what is the pattern with committee purchasing?

- Can you speak with members of the committee?

- How have the committee members interacted with one another in the past?

These questions serve to educate you on the company's purchasing process. There may be many people you pick up along the way, and this way can begin to resemble a maze. To untangle this maze, I encourage my salespeople to continue to ask question upon question of prospects. With each new buying influence that enters the maze, use appropriate questions to ferret out the information that delivers not only the Dominant Buying Influence but points to the path of the purchasing process.

Chapter Highlights

Chapter 5, Buying Influences

Simple or complex sale determines your approach

- Chauffeur: has a vested interest in your company earning the business.
- Investigative Buyer: gathers products /service information.
- Utilitarian Buyer: is the user of your product/service.
- Sensitive Buyer: is directly affected by results of the product or service.
- Dominant Buyer: dominates all other buying influences and has the final decision or money power.

Chapter 6

RESOURCES

The Salesperson's Money Fears

We have reached the point in the sales call where we have uncovered the prospect's emotional reasons for buying, have identified the appropriate buying influences, and are now faced with our next goal, which is to establish whether or not there are funds available to purchase our product or service. However, this is one of the most difficult areas for the salesperson. It sounds easy enough. Just ask if the company has the funds available to invest in your product or service. But how often have you balked at this point in the sales call? And why might that be? Do you still harbor an embarrassing memory of talking about someone else's money or worth? Are you afraid the prospect will be insulted if the question of available funds comes up? Shouldn't it simply be implied that the prospect is able to afford your product or service? After all, you were invited in to discuss products or services. But isn't it impolite for the salesperson to bring up money?

This may be the mindset of some individuals, so I'll teach you how to overcome those hesitancies.

Another reason for salespeople's inability to approach the money issue with a prospect is the belief they are not convinced of the value of the product or service they are selling. They may understand the working value of the product but may be afraid to discuss its worth with conviction in terms of the actual cost of the service or product. They do not want to be put in the position of defending the cost.

And finally, they may truly fear losing the business if the cost of the product or service is challenged. Do you really have the business until the money is in your pocket? Learn to be confident when defending the price of your product or service. Understand its value to the consumer, whose emotional response indicates a need for your service or product.

Terms

Too often, salespeople leave conversations about terms of payment to the accounting department. And because of this, the salesperson sees charge backs on their commission statements. How does this happen? It begins with the reticence to talk about money and consequently rolls over to a lapse in discussing the form of payment. It is so much easier to let the accounting department handle money collection. Of course, you are not the finance person; you merely collect the commission and do not worry about a payment plan for your client.

Here is what typically happens when a salesperson hands over the terms of payment to the accounting department instead of taking it up with the prospect. A company has a standard net 30-day payment plan and invoices the client. On the 45th day of the invoice, with no payment received, the dunning or collection letter goes out to the client. At 60 to 90 days past, the salesperson becomes involved and phones the client with a reminder that payment is 30 days net and the client is now three months overdue. It is a rare occurrence when the client quickly follows up with payment. Instead, the salesperson is likely to hear the client complain that he did not have a conversation about your company's payment schedule.

Where does the pressure fall? On the salesperson who has not defined his company's payment terms.

Suppose instead, that the salesperson discussed terms during the conversation about resources. This conversation will have a different tone. Instead of the client accusing the salesperson with a "You didn't tell me that!" statement, the salesperson asks the question, "What should we do now?" The pressure to commit to payment is back on the shoulders of the client, where it should be. Tired of charge backs? We hope so, because it is time you learn to take charge of the resources issue.

Starting a Resource Conversation

Now that you have an understanding of the salesperson's role in securing resource information and defining payment terms, how do you start the resource conversation?

Very simply, ask if there are resources available to fund this project. If you can put aside all the social taboos and muster the confidence you have in yourself and your product, you will find that there are three types of prospects that you will encounter: 1. those who have budgets or funding, 2. those who don't have budgets (Negative NOrman), and 3. those who may have budgets but refuse to divulge the information (Negative Ned).

Though all these answers appear to be rather straightforward, further questioning by the salesperson reveals more complicated scenarios.

The Prospect Who Has a Budget

The answer is "Yes"!

The follow-up question is, "Can you tell me approximately how much that might be?" Up to this point, the salesperson has qualified the prospect based on the level of trust achieved during the rapport stage, uncovered the prospect's emotional reasons for buying, heard the prospect define the problem's financial cost to the company, and now can expect to hear that the prospect is willing to invest in the product or service being offered. If the prospect has $1000 available and your product is $900, your response is, "I think we may be able to work with that."

If, on the other hand, the cost of the product is $5000, the salesperson knows there isn't enough money for the product, and the sales call ends. Remember, you, as the salesperson have invested the time of ONE sales call up to this point and can walk away now. Or you can further establish the financial qualifications of your candidate using the following comment.

"It doesn't sound as though you have enough resources to solve your problem."

If your prospect sincerely wants to solve the problem and indicates that finding resources is a possibility even though resources have not been budgeted, you can ask,

"Historically, what process did you or your company follow when you needed to find resources to pay for a solution?"

The salesperson will continue to question the prospect until the conversation reveals a clear understanding that resources can be secured and the salesperson is comfortable with the direction the sales call is going. Further questions will lead you up the food chain while you learn who else may be involved in approving the resources.

The Negative NOrman or The prospects With No Budget

This method of questioning can be applied to the second answer when the prospect says, "We don't have the budget to pay for your product or service." Why do we follow up with a prospect with no budget or resources? When a prospect has indicated a problem and appears to want to solve the problem, an assertive salesperson will follow up with, "You have a problem that you want to fix, so how were you hoping to fix it?"

If you hear from the prospect that resources are sometimes made available, you ask a question similar to the one in the previous budget paragraph. "Can you tell me approximately how much that might be?" That may well find you discovering new buying influences that do lead to available resources. Under these conditions, the salesperson must be assured that there is a clear understanding of fund approval. If resources don't appear to be available, then the sales call ends.

Negative Ned or The Prospect That May Have a Budget and is Reluctant to Reveal It

A prospect with an unwillingness to divulge information is an even bigger roadblock in the sales call. When a prospect does not wish to give out any financial information, the salesperson must decide if the prospect might still be viable and, if so, continue the conversation based on an agreement to ask a couple more questions. And though you do not need an exact figure from the prospect, you do need to determine financial ability to purchase. You do not want to spend your limited and precious resource – time--in a sales call that goes nowhere for lack of financial resources. In response to this prospect's unwillingness or inability to divulge financial information, the salesperson uses a ballpark-figure process. The salesperson wants to find out if the prospect has financial resources within a certain ballpark of the product or service available. To coax a prospect to reveal his resources, the salesperson prompts,

"Well, of course I can understand that you may not be able to tell me your available resources, but for me to understand if I should still be here, is your financial resource availability in the ballpark of $900 to $1000?"

Hopefully you will get agreement and can follow up with,

"Right now I'm not looking for an exact number. I'm just trying to figure out if I should be here or if there are others I need to speak with to approve the funds."

If the prospect is willing to grant this information to a range of availability, the sales call moves forward. The salesperson may also find that the prospect will never have the resources and will let you go.

You have heard three different answers to the question, "Do you or your company have financial resources available to purchase our product/service?" The stellar salesperson examines the possibilities of each answer supplied by a prospect and moves forward with questions appropriate to each answer. Stellar salespeople confident in their product/service will not be tempted to financially undersell just to make a sale and are usually fearless when asking a prospect if financial resources are available.

I had been working on a multimillion-dollar sale for three years with a Fortune 500 customer. The marketing team in the company had an emotional reason to buy, as their largest competitor had implemented a similar marketing solution sold by our company's largest competitor. The company claimed the competitive marketing program was the key reason they were losing sales and market share to the competitor. We implemented many trial programs, and after a three-year sales cycle they informed me they were ready to go and that our solution had the buy off at the highest levels. I asked how much had been budgeted, and they replied, don't worry about it –this is a strategic initiative for the company.

OK, I thought, it's rock and roll time! – I will have earned a place on our company's sales incentive trip to Switzerland with my wife, and my name will be in lights with our company after three years of hard work. This was my biggest sale ever. I could tell my wife to go shop for the new car she wanted. This sale was done. They said it was a done deal and they had budget.

Then I realized I needed to find out who approved the budget. The COO of this $50B company said our solution was a strategic initiative. I asked if the CFO had approved the sale, and the reply was, "Don't worry about the CFO, we have this handled."

I dropped work on all other piddling sales to ensure we locked up this sale. Once other decision makers were identified, I flew all over the country and met with other members of their marketing team.

I was certain we would get this big sale. We had a seventeen-projector multi-media, $30k presentation just to make sure everyone attending the presentation was excited. Competition was invited in to ensure the company was receiving a fair price. We had internal coaches working with us on the presentation, and the day before, we had them preview and give feedback on the presentation. The T's were crossed and the I's dotted; or were they?

We presented, and it was a fantastic presentation. "You nailed it!" were the comments and feedback we received from the 30+ attendees at the presentation. I was so confident that I had the agreement drawn up and presented to the team at the end of the presentation, with an estimated budget, since I wasn't able to obtain a budget number from the prospects. They claimed they were unable to divulge the budget numbers. We all thought we should charge more than usual, since it had been such a long sales cycle and was a strategic initiative for the company.

Days went by, and we received no signed agreement; all we heard was that it was in legal in review. Finally, after eleven business days and feeling like I had been to hell and back and was now pessimistic about the business, we got a response. "The executive team didn't have a budget set aside and decided that the solution was too much of a me-too response and we needed something radically different to differentiate our company."

How did I invest so much and get nothing? **We didn't ever confirm the budget or resources**. In this case the only executive who would confirm a budget was the CFO, and we believed the people we did meet with when they said not to worry about the CFO because "they had it handled." We never met with the CFO.

In another project in the mid-1980's, we were working to develop a sales incentive program for a large software company that sold through distributors. The program would motivate the distributors to sell more of the prospect's software. We tested the program with one distributor and initial results proved that for every dollar invested, the program produced over 200 for the company: that's over a 200 to 1 Return on Investment.

The prospect told me the results proved that this is a no-brainer sale and would be rolled out to the entire company. I announced the big sale to the executives in our company—the largest sale for our company that year. The software company needed to allocate budget to pay for the fixed program costs to get the program going and pay for the first half-year before reaping the returns. My prospect had just one more sign-off with the executive team of the company. The prospect said again that it was a no-brainer and just a formality and that everyone on the executive team endorsed the program.

The prospect presented to the executive team on a Thursday, and I didn't hear from him until the next

Tuesday. The opening words from him were, "Wow, I was blindsided." That didn't sound like an approval of the big sale. "I have bad news," he went on, "the CEO and CFO said we need a employee cafeteria in our Silicon Valley facility and must take the money earmarked for the incentive and put it into the employee cafeteria." How did that happen? A solid ROI improves company sales and they put in an employee cafeteria! Yes, it is a true story.

I clearly did not meet with all the Buying Influences to find out that no resources were ever really allocated to my company's program. Why? Because I didn't ask to meet with all buyers of the program or ask if $xxx, xxx was allocated in a budget to begin the program.

Chapter Highlights

Chapter 6, Resources

Identify the type of prospect you encounter:

1-Those with a budget

- Ask further questions.

- Qualify that there is sufficient budget for your company's solution.

2-Negative NOrman-those with no budget

- Ask questions to determine how to fix the problem or find out why you are meeting?

- Attempt to discover new buying influences.

3--Negative Ned –those who may have a budget and are unwilling to divulge the budget

- Ask for a ballpark budget.
- Determine if it is worthwhile to you and the prospect to continue discussions.

Chapter 7

Pre-Presentation Agreement (PPA)

Most salespeople make the mistake of not putting in place a Pre-Presentation Agreement (PPA). Without the PPA, the salesperson risks getting stuck in radio silence and losing control of the sale. This is a critical chapter for every salesperson.

In Chapter Two, we state that the value of any product or service a salesperson brings to the marketplace is equivalent to GOLD. Though its actual cost to the client may be anywhere from $100 to more than a $1,000,000, if that product/service can solve a problem for a client, it's value to the client is much greater than the dollar figure attached to it. Traditional selling models build the features and benefits presentation into the initial phase of the sales call giving the prospect almost immediate access to the salesperson's GOLD. One of the biggest missteps a salesperson can make is giving away the GOLD. Until a prospect is completely qualified, the prospect does not get access to the salesperson's GOLD. There needs to be a clear understanding of the prospect's ERB, a complete list of the buying influences, and sufficient resources and payment terms for the product/services.

By giving away the GOLD with a features and benefits presentation before completely qualifying the prospect, the salesperson ends up in a defensive position, haggling price, or in no position, with doors closing behind him. The salesperson loses control of the sale. Being certain to qualify the prospect is critical to the outcome of the sale and to the salesperson's maintaining control of the sale. In the previous chapters we outlined the methods for qualifying prospects.

- Establish Rapport, gauging the time wisely.
- Determine the ERB.
- Put in place a strong Meeting Agenda.
- Determine the Buying Influences.
- Mutually agree on the handling of Future Communications.
- Discuss Resources and Payment Terms.

At the final stage of qualifying the prospect, the salesperson is ready to deliver the solution with a well-prepared presentation of the product or service. The salesperson is ready to deliver the GOLD. But hold it. Not so fast. I see the salesperson as still in the READY – FIRE – AIM position. And you are probably thinking, "What else is there? I've covered all my bases. The prospect is financially qualified, and payment terms have been outlined."

There is one final item in the sales call arsenal to be employed before the salesperson delivers the GOLD. It is called the PRE-PRESENTATION AGREEMENT. Again, you are probably thinking, "I've had conversations to uncover the ERB. The Meeting Agenda is agreed upon. Financial resources are clearly available. I've checked my list and covered everything. Now what? Haven't I learned all the information necessary to close the deal?"

Throughout the qualifying process, the salesperson continually re-confirms all the points from the oral or written agenda and gets agreement from the prospect on those points. The prospect hears herself/himself give the "OK" to what has been agreed or understood. By revisiting each qualifier with the prospect, the salesperson creates a Feedback Loop that each party hears. Consider that 90% of the time spent in front of the prospect is in oral communications, which in turn means that the majority of the agreements reached between the prospect and salesperson are oral agreements.

It may seem redundant to some to use the Feedback Loop at this point, but think of the number of times in conversations with individuals that YOU have asked for clarification of points or expansion of ideas. It is not unusual for any of us to forget or misunderstand specific points of agreement during the course of oral communications. Though we all attempt to hear what another is saying, at the same time we often have thoughts and questions forming in our minds ready to be asked or exchanged when our next opportunity to speak occurs. We may miss another's point here or there in the conversation. We may selectively listen for information important to us and miss a point valuable to the other party.

The PPA is the last opportunity to employ the Final Feedback Loop before the presentation. The salesperson revisits each step in the sales call with the prospect to be certain the prospect has a clear understanding of what has been stated and agreed upon and more importantly has not forgotten any key points. This PPA further reinforces the likelihood that the meeting agreements will be kept and the sale will go through. Both the salesperson and the prospect are given the opportunity to clarify any points they may not have understood or include anything that may have been left out of the agreement. Without the PPA, the salesperson continues to withhold the GOLD.

- The PPA has seven steps that create a loop of information from the prospect back to the salesperson. At any point in the PPA the salesperson or the prospect has the opportunity to correct, clarify or expand the verbal/written agreement.

- Review the emotional reasons for buying.
- Confirm the financial resources are available to buy.
- Revisit the agreement with the prospect to either decline or accept the offer.

The salesperson is always searching for more emotional reasons for buying –ERBs. When we have been asked why the salesperson might need more ERBs, we always reply that we have never had a student come to me to say he just lost the deal because he got too many ERBs. It is also possible for a new buying influence to enter the picture. It is better now for the salesperson to have the information of another buying influence than to be surprised later when the sale falls apart because that buying influence is not on board.

Prospects can be fickle when money/ability to buy is discussed, so terms of payment need to be nailed down and be clear to all parties. Even after confirming agreement on all these important areas, the prospect still has the opportunity to decline the salesperson's offer. A prospect is always ready to put up barriers when dealing with a salesperson. The prospect removes that barrier of "being taken to the mat" by an aggressive salesperson when given permission to decline an offer of a product/service. From the prospect's perspective, the product or service may NOT be what is expected. It is important for both the prospect and the salesperson to be OK hearing "no thanks."

If a prospect does not make a decision either way, opting instead for more time to think about it, what should be the salesperson's next move? The assertive salesperson sees this tactic as prospect manipulation and calls him on it. By questioning the prospect on exactly what he needs to think about, the salesperson is likely to hear that the prospect:

- Doesn't want to buy and is trying to be nice.

- May be trying to get more information.

- Is still skeptical.

- May not be able to make a buying decision.

- May not have the resources to buy.

- May be afraid to make a buying decision.

Or the salesperson may not have the true ERB. If one of these roadblocks to a sale crops up, the salesperson needs to dig deeper. "Can we expand on that?" If another issue is discovered, it can be determined then whether the sales call can go forward or if it will end. The PPA is a critical element in the selling process. It reinforces and confirms the many oral or written agreements made in the sales interview. It lets the prospect see you as an active listener. It clears the way for the prospect to say no and reduces the likelihood of a "think it over." In closing, the rule is NO PRE-PRESENTATION AGREEMENT– NO GOLD.

Recently I was working with a digital marketing company to start up their sales. We had a sale that was in the bag at Big Software Company. The digital marketing company founders had given free trial copies of its product to the Big Software company and had announced to the Board of Directors and me that these sales were ready to be closed. They had zealous advocates of the company's products. At Big Software, the VP of Technology was the advocate and would filter news to us about the selling process at Big Software. His stated emotional reason for buying was that it would allow the Big Software Company to drive efficiencies out of recent company acquisition and provide a new product for Big Software to sell. As I got to know the VP, it was apparent that this wasn't an emotional reason for buying at all, and he wanted to throw some new initiatives out to prove his value and save his job. Clearly, I didn't understand the ERB and didn't have a precise picture of the financial implications of the sale. It also meant I hadn't confirmed that financial resources were available. I began to dig into the sale and identify other parties at Big Software who would be affected by the decision. We had yet to present the solution to the executive team or Dominant Buyer.

The VP wasn't introducing me, so I began setting up meetings on my own when I realized that I had yet to confirm and meet with all Buying Influences and that they had no knowledge of my company's digital marketing solution. It had the potential of billing $5 million per year. This company kept running a no-cost trial program with our company just to keep me coming around and buying lunch for them. We had built the framework for the sale based on the client's word that we would get the business. We told the client about all the secret sauce, intellectual property, or GOLD of the business, and in turn they promised we would get the business when that big day came for the executive presentation. Oh, and there will be fourteen people from all over the country that will be part of the presentation. Don't worry though, we have your backs (according to the VP), and, we are the only ones that matter in this decision.

The format for the presentation was based on the digital marketing and the secret sauce or GOLD from us. Crap, I thought, some clients pay money for this work, and did they send this information to our competitor? Yes, they had. I was upset, as we had given that to them in confidence, yet they shared it with a competitor.

According to my contact, "Don't worry, just present your recommendations. The approval is just a formality. You needn't meet with the other executives."

A week went by and no word from the client, always a bad sign. Another two days, no word. I called, and the client said, "Oh, nothing to worry about, we needed to invite in a competitor just to ensure we get a fair price. Standard company purchasing practices. Don't worry. You have the business. I know you have contacted other people in our company, and I will take care of you."

I called back two days later. "Hey, my trusted friend, what is the budget?" I had yet to establish there were available resources.

My prospect responded, "You need to come back with your best offer. That is part of the process."

"Will you give a ballpark budget amount to me?" I asked.

"You come back with your best price."

"Is $2-5 million in the range?"

"I guess so." he responded.

"Great," I said. "Our Company has been working on this for two years so it must be at least $2 million. I can accept the range." They did sound a bit sketchy and uncertain though.

Two weeks before the presentation I had lunch with my friends at Big Software Company who were taking care of my business, and they promised this would be a sale. We brought in their boss who could sign the checks and approve the budget; just to be certain that base was covered. He told me some news. My competitors are flying around and meeting with everyone on the presentation committee. And why wouldn't they? They have nothing to lose. "Don't worry though," he said, "My team has told me this business is yours."

Wow, this felt weird. My insiders had told me not to bother meeting with them. The CEO of my company even said it's wasteful to go meet with them and spend all the company money. He said, "We earned this business, and if that's what it takes, we don't want their business." I was feeling very uneasy by now.

I added three people on the day of the presentation from our company as a show of force. We laid out our recommendations, or GOLD, which is what the RFP is based on. The presentation went well, seemed to be smooth, lots of head nods. They knew we deserved this business and that we understood their company. The business was ours. Maybe. This was unfortunate, as the owners had given up all of this information before I was brought in and it is difficult to unravel.

Two days of waiting after the presentation for confirmation of the big sale. Two and a half days after the presentation I was still waiting for the call. Should I go to lunch and miss it? Friday afternoon at 2 p.m. and still no call. At 2:17 p.m. the phone rang, and it was the Big Software client. I was exhilarated and ready to accept the business, the big order.

They started out by saying, "You understand our business, and it was a great presentation. Your competitor gets the business." I felt betrayed and lied to and felt they stole our ideas. How could that be their response?

"You were out-sold," he told me. "Your competitor took your ideas and made them even better. They met with everyone on the committee, and their presentation addressed each individual and what their needs were. It was the best selling I have seen. Sorry about that."

There was only one consolation. My competitor never got the business because the budget was never approved. Within a month the VP and EVP of Big Software had left the company, and when I met with the Big Software COO, I discovered he had never been in favor of the initiative.

Unfortunately, that company's false assurances about this sale to our Board of Directors without a Pre-Presentation Agreement led to my departure and to that company's eventual demise.

Another time in another job I was calling on a major auto company in Detroit and working to get in position for a big sale in the fourth quarter to wrap up the year.

I had met with all the buyers and Buying Influences and had a clear understanding of the financial implications. They had agreed to say no or yes and had confirmed the emotional reason for buying, which was to be perceived as further ahead than their automotive competitors by consumers and their competitors. Prior to presenting, we had confirmed a budget amount. The client said they might say no if the budget wasn't approved, although they believed it would be approved, and typically it had been approved in the past. We also had met with the budget approver. They all liked our solution and said they would approve the budget. I found the actual budget approver by asking the manager I had been working with, who gave me a heads-up on the budget question. The question I asked to gain that introduction was, "If you like our solution, what happens then?" He said I would need to meet with the budget approver. I told my contact that if he wanted the benefits of our solution, he would need to arrange and attend the meeting with the budget approver and me. In the meeting with the budget approver, I prepped the manager and had him state his financial implications and emotional reason for buying.

I then asked the budget approver if he allocated the budget for our solution, and he said yes. I asked if he would say no if there wasn't a match. He stated that from all he heard, it sounded like there was a match. So I said it sounded like a yes and I asked him if there were anyone else that we needed to meet with or any other issues that could stop this from being approved and what were the next steps? He replied that it would take about three weeks for the budget to be allocated to us. We scheduled a follow-up meeting and lunch three weeks later.

The prospect /Senior Vice President said the budget was approved; we sat down to lunch. and he filled out the order form. I had the CEO of our company with me, and he said that was the easiest sale he had ever seen. It was because I went through the PPA with the prospect, and then they found additional budget dollars. They had only allocated a smaller budget for our company and now had an additional $50,000 that had to be spent with our company by year's end. The PPA helped to secure the sale, and by securing the sale we were in the right place at the right time to receive more from their budget.

Chapter Highlights

Chapter 7 Pre-Presentation Agreement (PPA)

- Review the emotional reasons for buying.
- Confirm the financial implications of the problem.
- Confirm that financial resources are available to buy.
- Get an agreement from the prospect to say "no" if the product/service does not solve the problem.
- Get an agreement from the prospect to say "yes' if the product does solve the problem.
- Take it as a "no," if prospect asks to think it over.
- Make an agreement for ongoing communications.

Chapter 8

The Presentation

In the first chapter, we laid out the six-step format for sales' calls and now have arrived at the sixth step. This is the moment most salespeople anticipate and relish. The salesperson is ready to offer the solution to the problem and put an end to the prospect's pain.

Up to this point in the sales process, the salesperson has not spent a great deal of time talking about the product or service. The job in the initial stages of the selling process has been mainly to obtain information about the prospects emotional reasons for buying, discovering the buying influences, and knowing the availability of resources.

Now it's time to deliver the GOLD. The salesperson schedules a presentation time, collects the needed materials and allows sufficient time for review of the pre-presentation agreement and follow-up questions from the prospects.

The presentation typically focuses on the features and benefits of the product or service offered. However, features and benefits are often numerous, and not all may necessarily apply specifically to the prospect's problem. The salesperson that has learned the prospect's emotional reasons for buying is going to carefully tailor the presentation to maximize the impact to the prospects of the product's solution to the ERB.

Take for example a prospect that is purchasing a new car. The salesperson points out a number of features on a car, focusing on a particular model with the highest-rated air-conditioning unit. The prospect announces that he's taking the car to Barrow, Alaska, and has no need for the unit and is unlikely to pay extra for a feature that will have little or no value to him in that climate. By pointing out those features that have little value to the prospect before determining what the prospect's reasons for buying were, the salesperson has paid dearly.

The salesperson is ready and has worked hard to reach this step in the process. So just prior to the actual presentation, I teach my students to re-confirm all the points in the pre-presentation and to listen carefully for any Early Warning Indicators, EWI, that may pop up. If any appear, I tell them to settle the matter before moving on to the presentation, to avoid what happened to the over-eager car salesperson. Now is the time to deal with any issue that might stall the sale. When the prospect confirms again that he is ready for the solution, the salesperson is ready to make the presentation and begins with the question,

"Which of the issues affecting the business would you like to address first?"

Sometimes a reminder or refresher is required for busy executives. Did they mention that saving money was an important issue or that adding the new software with a 10 to 1 ROI is important? Are those the issues affecting their business that they would like to address first, has that changed, or are there other priorities and issues?

By giving the prospect the opportunity to prioritize the ERB issues, the salesperson allows a sense of control to move to the prospect. And the salesperson's presentation then hits the specific ERB points outlined by the prospect. The presentation stays focused on only those points specific to this sale.

After the presentation, we ask, "Based on the information just presented, are you completely satisfied that we can solve this problem for you?"

If there is any hesitation or they are less than completely satisfied, we ask, "Help me understand what would make you completely satisfied?" It may be that we need to spend more time answering questions, but I want to know while I am still in front of the prospect that this solution is sold. Spending this time now eliminates a stall.

When the time has come to close, I ask one last question, "Would you like our help?" And then I stop talking

Chapter Highlights

Chapter 8 The Presentation

- Tailor the presentation to maximize the impact of the product's solution to client's pain.
- Ask, "Which of the issues affecting the business would you like to address first?'
- Determine, based on the information presented, is the prospect completely satisfied that we can solve this problem?
- Finish with, "Would you like our help?"

Chapter 9

Confirmation

The new customer has done all the research, listened to all the competitors, and made the final decision to buy. The anticipation and excitement of purchasing a solution or new product to influence the bottom line has the customer riding a new high. This is often a short-lived high, though, before buyers' remorse rears its ugly head and the salesperson finds himself with a handwringing customer, questioning his recent investment. In order to avoid this practically inevitable occurrence, the salesperson must address these second thoughts immediately, and confirm the sale once again.

Buyer's Remorse

The salesperson understands that his product or service is not absolutely perfect, but the customer at the time of purchase believes it is. Before the customer faces buyer's remorse, the salesperson asks the customer to reflect on his decision to purchase. When re-examining the decision with the customer, a successful salesperson tends to ask questions such as:

- "What do you see as its greatest benefit?
- Where does it fit in your company?
- How will it be accepted? Why will it be useful?
- Are there any drawbacks to the product?
- Can you overcome the drawbacks?
- Will the drawbacks be significant?
- How will you address concerns, if any?

Asking these questions will ensure the sale stays intact.

Ward Off the Competition

Business does not exist without competition. Your competition is at your heels every day, which means that your prospect is also forced to deal with the competition. In most cases, the competition invariably works to dislodge your sale. My goal to secure the sale relies on my ability to help the prospect be comfortable and confident when approached by the competition. The salesperson asks the customer to tell why he bought from us. By telling why he bought from us, he reinforces his own buying decision. This in turn allows him to become less vulnerable to the inevitable attack from the competition.

Not all prospects need help in dealing with the competition, but preparing those who may be less confident when standing up to the competition further assures a confirmation of the sale.

Early in my career I was selling Performance Programs to companies. These were incentives and training programs. We competed for six months on an opportunity to sell and deliver a training program to employees at a major hotel company wishing to deliver world-class guest or customer service. What was behind the large initiative is that Hotel Company was positioning the company for sale and wanted to show they had world-class guest services. Our company was small and relatively unknown, and we were competing with some of the most renowned training companies. There was a committee of six people responsible for the decision.

There was a new executive responsible for HR who was the key decision maker or Dominant Buyer. She also brought in a cadre of people she worked with in previous companies, hoping to make a name in Customer or Guest Services. Our sale was very much driven by the influence of the relationship I had with the executive team. And at the time it appeared that the HR team went along with that team's decision to choose our company, albeit reluctantly.

I met with the team responsible for the implementation of the initiative and asked for the reasons they are doing business with our company. They said they were told to work with us and could actually do this project themselves. Our assumption was that despite their reluctance, we had cover from the executive team, and the VP of Sales said, "Let's get going—we need the revenue." When I asked what they would like from the solution that we had yet to present or what wasn't perfect about our solution, the implementation group said, "We need to be more involved." No problem, I thought, a very active client.

When I asked what they would say if any of our competitors came back, they stated, "We won't be working with any other outside firm."

We received a letter of intent and began our work with the hotel chain to design and build a world-class training program. I was traveling to Kansas City for the program kick-offs in the first week and received a call that the program was being pulled. The HR implementation team didn't see the value in the price tag and was pulling the program and would do it all themselves. I pleaded and cajoled, but no one in the company could turn it around.

I neglected to understand the importance of the new team and failed to convince them of the value of working with our group. I heard them tell me that they would bring the business in-house. Our company had over $10,000 in expenses and a lot of my time and got no business. In this case, I didn't understand the competition was internal resources. We didn't sell the value to the entire team and didn't really understand or want to understand the importance of confirmation in an agreement. In addition, we did not confirm an agreement that they would pay us in a timely manner for our services.

Chapter Highlights

Chapter 9, Confirmation

- Buyers Remorse- prevents the buyer from changing their mind.

- Warding Off the Competition prevents the competition from getting back in with the customer and stealing the sale from you.

The sale is not complete until you have delivered your product or service and the money is in your pocket.

Chapter 10

Summary

We wrote this book as a teaching tool for the many salespeople who find themselves frustrated with the traditional selling methods promoting product knowledge and a one-size-fits-all solution. Within that old framework, the salesperson is often flagged by the prospect as dishonest, slick, and at worst a liar. Yet so often it is the salesperson who is deceived or feels deceived by the prospect.

Our strategies for developing successful salespeople undo those old stereotypes. Understanding the selling process, learning to take control of the selling process, and mastering the steps to a successful sale provide a winning formula for both parties in a sale. The salesperson is confident that the money for his efforts will be in the bank, and the clients know they will receive a solution for their problem. The goodwill generated by two satisfied parties leads to a successful future in sales. We hope that in the end you will be a better listener, a better communicator, and a professional who realizes that what is hoped for in a sale is always that both parties win.

Bibliography

1. Bach, Richard. *Jonathan Livingston Siegel*: Avon, 1976.
2. Bandler, Richard, and Grinder, John. *Frogs Into Princes*: Real People Press, 1979.
3. Bandler, Richard and Grinder, John. *Using Your Brain For A Change:* Real People, 1985.
4. Bettger, Frank. *How I Raised Myself From Failure to Success in Selling*: Simon & Shuster, 1947.
5. Bosworth, Michael. *Solution Selling*: McGraw–Hill, 1994.
6. Buzotta, Lefton. *Effective Selling Through Psychology*: Ballinger, 1965.
7. Carnegie, Dale. *How To Win Friends and Influence People*: Pocket Books, 1936.
8. Hartman, Thom. *Cracking The Code*: Berrett-Koehler Publishers, Inc., 2007.
9. Hogan, Evin. The Psychology of Persuasion: Pelican Publishing, 1966.
10. Hogan, Evin. *The Science of Influence*: John Wiley & Sons, Inc., 2005.
11, Hill, Napoleon. *Think and Grow Rich*: Combined Registry Co., 1937.
12. Jolles, Rob. *Customer Centered Selling*: Free Press, 2000.
13. Konrath, Jill. *SNAP Selling*: Penguin Group, 2010.
14. Kurlan, Dave. *Baseline Selling*: authorhouse, 2005.
15. Laborde, Genie. *Influencing With Integrity*: Dell, 1989.
16. Mandingo, Og. *The Greatest Miracle In The World*: Frederick Fell, 1977.
17. Meyer, Paul. *The Power of Goal Setting*: Success Motivation Institute, 1960.
18. Morgan, Sharon Drew. *Selling With Integrity*: Berkeley Press, 1999.
19. Peale, Norman Vincent. *The Power of Positive Thinking*: Prentice Hall, 1952.
20. Rackham, Neal. *Spin Selling*: McGraw–Hill, 1988.
21. Robbins, Anthony. *Unlimited Power*: Free Press, 1985.

22. Robert III, Martyn. *Robert's Rules of Order*: Da Capo Press, 1876.

23, Stone, W. Clement. *The System That Never Fails:* Prentice Hall, 1962.

24. Wheeler, Elmer. *How to Sell Yourself to Others*: Dell, 1947.

25. Wheeler, Elmer. *Tested Sentences That Sell*: Prentice Hall, 1935.

26. White, Wendall. *The Psychology of Dealing*: The McMillan, 1936.

Glossary

Ballpark range– the process of learning the minimum to maximum resources available to purchase.

Bandwidth --In business jargon, the resources needed to complete a task or project.

Buying Influences – Individuals with decision-making authority.

CFO – Chief Financial Officer.

CEO – Chief Executive Officer.

COO – Chief Operating Officer.

CRM – Customer Relationship Management.

Charge Back – negative dollar charges against a commission statement.

Chauffeur - a person inside the prospects company who helps a salesperson through the selling process.

Commission Statement - statement of earned commissions.

Complex sale – a sale that has high dollar value and multiple buying influences. Generally has a long selling cycle.

Confirmation - confirming the sale with the customer

Dominant Buyer – the principal buying influence. Can trump other buying influences by saying yes or no.

Dynamic positioning statement – a short statement identifying the type of customers a salesperson works with, what specifically they do for their customers, and a third-party report about the results their customers experience as a result of using the salesperson's product or service.

Early Warning Indicator – a signal from the prospect of problem to be solved. See Ch. 4

ERB - emotional reason(s) for buying.

EVP - executive vice president.

GOLD - the potential value of the salesperson's products/services in the marketplace.

Investigative Buyer - the individual who researches products and services for their company.

Meeting Agenda – a written or oral agreement between the salesperson and the prospect that defines the outcome of the sales call.

Moment of Choice – the point in the sales call that determines which party will control the sale.

Pre-Presentation Agreement – A review of all the factors influencing the sale. See Ch. 7.

Radio Silent – when the prospect no longer communicates with the salesperson.

Resources – the amount of money available to purchase the salespersons product or service.

RFP - Request For Proposal.

RFQ - Request For Quote.

ROI – return on monetary investment.

Sensitive Buyer – the individual within a company most likely to suffer from the consequences of not having the salesperson's product/service.

Signing Authority aka Dominant Buyer – person who has the authority to sign the order.

Social Media – web-based and mobile technologies used to turn communication into interactive dialogue.

Terms - agreed-upon payment method.

T I O - Think It Over.

VP – Vice President.

Simple Sale – a low-dollar volume sale. Typically has one to two buying influences and is generally a short sale cycle.

Solution – the answer to the Emotional Reason for Buying.

Utilitarian Buyer – the primary user of the salesperson's product/service.

Contact: james.hayden@comcast.net